WORLD CULTURES
Aleuts

STEVE GOLDSWORTHY

MEDIA ENHANCED BOOKS
AV2 BY WEIGL™
ADDED VALUE • AUDIO VISUAL

www.av2books.com

Go to **www.av2books.com**, and enter this book's unique code.

BOOK CODE

R638992

AV² by Weigl brings you media enhanced books that support active learning.

AV² provides enriched content that supplements and complements this book. Weigl's AV² books strive to create inspired learning and engage young minds in a total learning experience.

Your AV² Media Enhanced books come alive with...

Audio
Listen to sections of the book read aloud.

Key Words
Study vocabulary, and complete a matching word activity.

Video
Watch informative video clips.

Quizzes
Test your knowledge.

Embedded Weblinks
Gain additional information for research.

Slide Show
View images and captions, and prepare a presentation.

Try This!
Complete activities and hands-on experiments.

... and much, much more!

Published by AV² by Weigl
350 5th Avenue, 59th Floor
New York, NY 10118
Website: www.av2books.com   www.weigl.com

Library of Congress Cataloging-in-Publication Data
Goldsworthy, Steve.
  Aleuts / Steve Goldsworthy.
    pages cm. -- (World cultures)
  Summary: "Facts about the Aleut indigenous peoples of northern Alaska and Russia. Includes information about their traditions, myths, social activities, the development of their culture, methods of hunting and gathering, rituals, and their daily lives. Intended for fifth to eighth grade students"--Provided by publisher.
  ISBN 978-1-62127-511-4 (hardcover : alk. paper) -- ISBN 978-1-62127-515-2 (softcover : alk. paper)
  1. Aleuts--Juvenile literature. I. Title.
  E99.A34G65 2014
  979.8'401--dc23
                        2013000849

Printed in the United States of America in North Mankato, Minnesota
1 2 3 4 5 6 7 8 9 0 17 16 15 14 13

052013
WEP040413

Project Coordinator   Aaron Carr
Art Director   Terry Paulhus

Photo Credits
Every reasonable effort has been made to trace ownership and to obtain permission to reprint copyright material. The publishers would be pleased to have any errors or omissions brought to their attention so that they may be corrected in subsequent printings.

Weigl acknowledges Getty Images as its primary image supplier for this title. Other sources: Alaskastock: pages 5, 11, 14, 15, 17, 18, 20. Alamy: pages 8 and 9. iStockphoto: pages 21 and 27.

CONTENTS

Where in the World?

RUSSIA

ALASKA

Bering Sea

Gulf of Alaska

Shumagin Islands

Aleutian Islands

PACIFIC
OCEAN

ATLANTIC
OCEAN

SOUTH
AMERICA

LEGEND
Aleut distribution

N
W E
S
SCALE

0   200 kilometers

0   200 miles

Population:
  U.S. – 315.1 million
  RUSSIA – 141.9 million
**Indigenous Population
(Aleuts):**
  approximately
  15,000 worldwide
Continent: North America
  and Europe
States: Alaska, U.S.
Territories:
  Far Eastern Russia
Area: 6,821 square
  miles (17,666
  square kilometers)

The story of the Aleut people is a story of survival. The Aleuts inhabit one of the harshest environments on Earth. They are an **indigenous** people of the Aleutian Islands of Alaska. These islands stretch westward more than 1,200 miles (1,931 km) from the Alaskan Peninsula, across the Northern Pacific Ocean to the Kamchatka Peninsula in Russia.

Today, more than 17,000 people identify themselves as being of Aleutian descent. Only about 2,000 of them are directly related to the earliest people from this area, the ancient Paleo-Aleuts. The name "Aleut" comes from the Aleut word *allíthuh* meaning "community."

The Aleuts have faced great challenges in their history. Many of these issues began when European fur traders moved into the territory more than 200 years ago. In recent decades, the Aleuts have had to adjust their way of life in order to survive. Environmental issues, such as **climate change** and oil spills, have also threatened the Aleut population.

Traditionally, tattooing is an important form of self-expression for Aleut people. Younger Aleut women often enhance their own personal beauty by pricking designs on their cheeks, chins, or upper lips.

Culture Cues

◎ Alaska is the largest state by area in the United States at 663,323 square miles (1,718,000 sq. km). It is larger than England, France, Italy, and Spain combined. Alaska has the lowest population density of any state at 1.2 people per square mile (2.59 sq. km).

◎ The Alaskan city with the largest population is Anchorage, with almost 295,000 people. That is more than 40 percent of the state's entire population. Anchorage is the northernmost city in the United States.

Alaska's capital city, Juneau, cannot be accessed by road from the rest of the state as it is surrounded by water and mountains.

◎ In 2011, the population of Alaska was made up of 67.9 percent Caucasian, 3.6 percent African American, 5.6 percent Asian, and 11.6 percent other races. American Indians made up 14.9 percent. Pacific Islanders, such as the Aleuts, accounted for 1.1 percent of the population. Ethnic groups related to the Aleuts include the Inuit, Yupik, Sirenik, and Sadlermiut.

Stories and Legends

The Aleutian Islands are a beautiful, natural landscape. Most of the islands' land is undeveloped.

The Aleut people have a long history of storytelling. Many of their legends and myths, however, have been lost or forgotten. When **missionaries** arrived in the 1800s, they began **converting** the Aleuts to Russian Orthodox Christianity. The missionaries discouraged the telling of the Aleut stories and legends.

The early Aleuts practiced animism. Animism is a belief that things in the natural world have souls or are inhabited by spiritual beings. Everything from stones and trees to rivers and wind has a spirit. The ancient Aleuts prayed to these spirits and performed many ceremonies in their honor.

The early Aleuts believed in the creator god Agugux. His name means "creator" in early Aleut language. Agugux is the creator of all the Aleut tribes.

Most Aleut stories and legends involve hunting and maintaining balance with nature. In many stories, animals like the Great White Faced Bear warn the Aleut people not to over hunt animals. The trickster spirit of the Raven teaches the Aleut to live in harmony with the natural world.

The wilderness of the Aleutian Islands is home to animals such as bears and salmon. These animals play a major role in the people's myths and stories.

THE CREATION OF
The Four Winds

Once there was an Aleut couple who longed for a child. The moon spirit Iguluk came to the woman in a dream, telling her to find a sacred tree and make a doll from it. The woman's husband found this tree after searching along a bright path of moonlight. He chopped down the tree and made a small doll, some toy bowls, a spear, and a knife. The couple laid the doll in a place of honor by the door. They filled the bowls with food and water. The next morning, the doll was gone. The doll traveled along the path of moonlight to the four corners of the sky. He found four separate holes in the sky covered with animal skin. He sliced each skin open, releasing winds that carried animals and birds, as well as rainstorms and ocean waves. The doll returned to his village, bringing with him good fortune. The winds brought the animals and birds to hunt, and churned up the seas bringing sea mammals for the people. Aleut still make dolls like this today to continue their good fortune.

The earliest people to arrive in the Aleutian Islands were the Paleo-Aleuts. They arrived from the Alaskan mainland around 2000 BC. Some **archaeologists** think there may have been people on the islands for more than 7,000 years. The Paleo-Aleuts settled on the shorelines of the islands. Villages were established near fresh water supplies. These locations were good spots to land boats and provided protection against enemy attacks. Besides the Aleutian Islands, the Aleut people lived on the Shumagin Islands and the western part of the Alaskan Peninsula.

At the time of first contact with Europeans in the mid 1700s, the Aleutian population was around 25,000. That number dwindled to less than 2,000 by the end of the 19th century. Many Aleutians died as a result of diseases introduced to their population by Russian fur traders. When the traders arrived in the early 18th century, they established settlements on several islands. At first, the Russians traded with the Aleuts for otter **pelts**. Later, the fur traders began to exploit the Aleuts. They offered the Aleuts fewer goods in return for the furs. In some cases, the Russians enslaved the Aleut people.

Timeline of the Aleuts

1741
Danish explorer Vitus Bering discovers the Aleutian Islands.

1788
Russian fur traders enslave Aleuts, forcing them to hunt seals.

1834
Aleut population decreases by more than 90 percent, but 27 Aleut villages remain throughout the Aleutian Islands.

1808
Alaska's first Russian Orthodox Church is constructed. Many Aleut begin converting to the Christian religion.

They moved large groups of Aleuts to the Pribilof Islands. There the Aleuts were forced to hunt for marine animals. Many Aleutians fought back. In 1784, a group of them rose up against Russian workers on the island of Amchitka. The Russians were able to scare off more than 100 Aleut men who came to attack the workers' houses. Four Aleut leaders were executed for their part in the **revolt**.

Russian Christian missionaries began arriving in the Aleutian Islands in the mid 1800s. One of the first was a Russian Orthodox priest named Ivan Veniaminov, who arrived with his family in 1824. He learned the Aleut language and began converting many Aleuts to Russian Orthodox Christianity.

During World War II, the Japanese invaded the Aleutian Islands, occupying Attu and Kiska Islands. They captured some Aleutian Islanders on Attu and held them as prisoners of war. The U.S. government evacuated 820 Aleuts from neighboring islands to remove them from the war zone and placed them in **internment** camps in southeast Alaska. Many Aleutians died in these camps.

1878
The Western Fur and Trading Company establishes a trading port on Akutan Island.

1942
The Japanese invade the Aleutian Islands of Attu and Kiska.

1971
The Aleut Corporation is formed to settle land claims by the Aleut people.

1912
Alaska becomes a territory of the United States.

1959
Alaska becomes a U.S. state.

1998
The Aleut International Association is established to address issues facing Arctic indigenous people such as the Aleut.

Social Structures

Early Aleut villages were ruled by chiefs. Sometimes one chief would rule over several villages on one island. An Aleut chief's rule was not based on brute strength or a warrior's dominance. It was based on his wisdom and ability to unite his people. He was a respected leader in the community, wise and experienced.

Aleut society had several levels. At the top were the village nobles, then the commoners, and finally the slaves. Chiefs were selected from the noble classes. Nobles' homes held a place of honor in the village. Their dwellings were larger than others and located in central, well-protected areas.

A death mask was placed over the face of a deceased shaman to prevent the spirit returning to revive the corpse before it could be buried.

Elders also were well respected. They passed on many of their stories and traditions to the younger generation.

Another important member of the Aleut community was a spiritual leader known as a shaman. This shaman was a holy man who interpreted signs from the spirit world. He healed the sick, read signs in nature that foretold the future, advised village leaders on hunting and warfare, and performed many religious ceremonies.

Early Aleuts believed the east was a sacred direction because that is where the sun rises. The east was also associated with their creator, Agugux. In the morning, Aleut men would face the east, greet the day, and "swallow light," or take in the sunshine.

In death, many Aleut were **mummified**. Their bodies were drawn up in a crouching position with their legs tucked under their arms. They were often buried in a sitting position and placed in a hole not far from their home.

Today, most Aleuts follow the Christian religion of Russian Orthodoxy. Many Aleuts have become priests and lead their people in worship.

There are more than 90 Russian Orthodox churches in the state of Alaska, and many of those are located in the Aleutian Islands.

Many of the Russian Orthodox churches in Alaska were built in the 19th century.

Saluting the Light

Early Aleut men observed the daily morning ritual of "Saluting the Light." At daybreak, they would emerge from their huts, approach the water, and strike it with their hands. Then they would say to the rising sun, "I am not asleep; I am alive; I greet with you the life-giving light, and I will always live with you."

Communication

The majority of Aleuts speak either English or Russian, depending on where they live. The Aleut language is a dying language. It is spoken by less than 150 people. It is part of the Eskimo-Aleut language family. There are three **dialect** groupings within the family. People speak Eastern Aleut on the Eastern Aleutian, Shumagin, Fox, and Pribilof islands. Atkan is spoken on the Atka and Bering Islands. The third dialect, called Attuan, is now extinct. On Bering Island, the Aleuts speak a mixture of Russian and Attuan called Copper Island Aleut.

The Russian Orthodox priest Ivan Veniaminov was one of the first Europeans to learn the Aleut language. He was the first person to translate their language to Russian.

Veniaminov created the first written alphabet of the Aleut language. He worked closely with Aleut chief Ivan Pan'kov to write the first book in an Alaskan Native language.

The Aleuts have a strong tradition of oral storytelling. Before Europeans introduced a written language to the Aleuts, the early Aleuts passed on their history from generation to generation through storytelling. Elders told of ancient legends involving sacred animals or the elements of wind, water, and the Sun. The Aleuts communicated through song and dance as well.

Aleut language expert Knut Bergsland studied the Aleut language for several decades, beginning in the 1950s. He worked with the Aleut to develop a modern writing system for the Aleut language. He also created a school dictionary for the Atkan dialect.

Today, Aleutian cultural groups sing songs in Aleut languages for special ceremonies.

Hello	*Aang*	I'm fine, thanks, and you?	*Maqagilakuq, qagaasal ama txin?*
Do you speak Aleut?	*Unangam tunuu Aadazaxt ii?*	What's your name?	*Kiin asax̂tax̂t?*
How are you?	*Alqutaxt/Alqutaltxin? Alqutaadaltxin?*	Sorry	*Amtal*
		Thank you	*Qaĝaasakung*
		Goodbye	*Ukudigada*

Law and Order

Before the Russians came to the Aleutian Islands, the Aleut people were made up of dozens of tribes that covered the islands. Tribes lived in villages ruled by a *toyuk*, or chief. There was often a second chief, called a sukaskiq. When Russian missionaries came to spread Russian Orthodox Christianity, the Aleuts created a *staritaq*. A *staritaq* was a chief who spoke both Aleut and Russian.

To solve conflicts between tribes, Aleut councils were held. Each village sent representatives to speak at the councils. The ruling chiefs quickly worked out their disagreements at these meetings. Despite this, however, the Aleuts sometimes raided other villages on neighboring islands. Sometimes, they attacked because they were seeking revenge for a past wrong. Often, any prisoners they captured during a raid would be brought back to their village to be used as servants.

The U.S. government purchased Alaska and the Aleutian Islands from the Russians in 1867. The Aleuts came under the **jurisdiction** of the United States and were forced to follow the rules and laws of that country.

Indigenous Peoples of the Aleutian Islands have fought for the right to continue their traditional whale hunting practices.

U.S. government agencies help to protect the environment and wildlife of the Aleutian Islands.

In 1971, the Alaska Native Claims Settlement Act was passed. It guaranteed certain land rights to the Aleuts. They received land and money in the settlement while allowing the U.S. government to drill for oil on Aleut land. The Aleut Corporation was founded a year later. It developed businesses in government contracting, telecommunications, oil and gas investment, real estate, and environmental protection.

Many of the Aleuts' rights and freedoms have been given special consideration by the U.S. government. Their beliefs are protected under the American Indian Religious Freedom Act created in 1978. Government groups such as the Commission on Wartime Relocation and Internment of Civilians have paid money to survivors of the internment camps of World War II.

Celebrating Culture

Masks are a traditional craft of the Aleuts. Early Aleuts created ornate masks from different materials. Masks have different meanings and are worn for different purposes.

The ceremonial season for the early Aleuts was from December through April each year. Many celebrations and festivals were held during this period. In these ceremonies, dancers moved to the beat of drums made from animal skins. Drummers beat their instruments with wooden sticks. Women and older men wore ceremonial hats, clothing, and masks. They shook rattles made from inflated seal stomachs. After the ceremonial season, the drums, rattles, and masks were broken and placed in caves, never to be used again. Many Aleuts today still celebrate in traditional dress and play music using these instruments.

The Aleuts found many ways to express themselves and their culture. Body piercing served a spiritual purpose for Aleuts. They believed that spots like the mouth, nose, and ears were places evil spirits could enter the body. By piercing these areas, they were stopping these entities, which they called *Khoughkh*. A few days after a baby's birth, the Aleuts would insert a nose pin in the baby's nose. These pins were made of bone, bark, or sometimes an eagle feather. Over time, women added pieces of amber and coral to the pin so it would hang down over their mouths.

Men pierced their ears with sea lion whiskers to prove their might as hunters. Lower lips were pierced with walrus tusks, beads, and bone. The more piercings a person had, the more that person was respected by other Aleuts.

Tattooing was an important form of self-expression for the Aleut people. Tattoos were a sign of social status and spiritual authority for some Aleuts. Aleut men received their first tattoo once they had killed their first animal. For early Aleut women, tattooing was a way to enhance their personal beauty. Young women pricked designs on their cheeks, chins, or upper lips as a sign of social class. When Russian traders arrived on the Aleutian Islands in the 18th century, they discouraged the tradition of tattooing, saying the practice took away from a woman's natural beauty. Today, few Aleuts practice tattooing or piercing their bodies. Instead, they use makeup to recreate these traditions for special ceremonies.

Some early Aleut drums were made from reindeer hides and wood.

Today, Aleut celebrations often include traditional singing, dancing, food, games, and storytelling.

Art and Culture

The Aleuts have a strong tradition of art. They have their own distinct style of weaving, carving, and figurine and mask making. They are well known for their unique ivory and wood carving. The subjects of these carvings included seals, whales, and people. Aleuts on various islands have their own unique styles. The early Aleuts traded their sculptures with Europeans for goods they could not obtain on the islands. They also traded with other Native Alaskan cultures. The Aleuts also carved beautiful jewelry out of ivory.

Each region of the Aleutian Islands has its own distinct style of wood carving.

The early inhabitants of the Aleutian Islands used baleen, or whalebone, to craft baskets.

Aleut women have a long tradition of basket weaving. Many still create beautiful, handcrafted baskets woven from dune wild rye grass. They call these grass baskets *qiigam aygaaxsii*. They also use birch tree bark and feathers. The Aleut art of basketry dates back to prehistoric times. Only Aleut women did basketry. Their only tools were their especially long and sharp thumbnails. Besides baskets, the women also made mats.

Masks were sacred to the early Aleut people. The Aleuts of Atka Island created masks to represent the ancient people they believed lived in the region long before they did. Other Aleut masks were a combination of human and animal faces. Most masks were carved from wood and decorated with paint made from berries, flowers, and ground stone. Some masks were also decorated with feathers.

Jewelry

Jewelry was an important part of Aleut life. Each tribe had its own distinct style of jewelry. Some tribes used stone. Others used animal bones and ivory. Often, they sculpted specific animals into the jewelry to represent their tribes. This way, the early Aleuts could tell what tribe someone belonged to based on his or her jewelry. Jewelry also represented an Aleut's social status within a tribe.

Dressing Up

The harsh conditions of the Aleutian Islands have had a strong influence on Aleut clothing. With temperatures well below freezing in the winter months, warmth is the number one priority for clothing. Aleuts today wear modern clothing that they buy from clothing stores. Early Aleuts, however, used natural resources from their environment to make their clothes. A traditional Aleut coat called a sax was made from bird skin and otter fur. Aleut men wore **parka** coats made from the skin of birds such as puffins. They wore the parkas with the feather side in and the skin side out, to create a warm, watertight barrier from the elements. In warmer weather, they flipped the parka inside out. When hunting on the water, they wore waterproof coats made from the stomachs and intestines of sea lions, bears, walrus, or whales. Aleut women made caps and parkas for their children from animal skins.

Early Aleut women wore sea otter fur parkas that extended below the knee.

Today, Aleut women wear traditional clothing for cultural performances.

Men brought back the skins of harbor seals and sea otters from the hunt. First, the skins were soaked and stretched. Then, the early Aleuts used a bone knife to prepare the animals' intestines. They cut the intestines, stretched them, and dried them on stakes. These were used for waterproof bags.

Women made sewing needles out of the wing bones of seabirds. Thread came from the **sinew** of animals. It took up to a year and 60 puffin skins to make one adult parka. Parkas were decorated with bird feathers, sea otter fur, dyed leather, and caribou hair.

Chaguda-x

A unique piece of Aleut dress is the chaguda-x, a traditional wooden hunting hat. Aleut craftsmen carved slabs of wood into thick sheets. These sheets were then steamed over hot water and bent over molds. They would form a kind of **visor** that fit over the front of a person's head. The hats were colorfully decorated with sea lion whiskers, feathers, and ivory. Some artisans still make these hats today.

Food and Fun

Early Aleuts fished for salmon, cod, crab, shellfish, walrus, and whale. They dried or roasted these foods. The **blubber** from whale and walrus was boiled and eaten as a delicacy. On land, Aleuts hunted caribou, moose, deer, and musk oxen. They also mixed dried berries with animal fat and fish. They called this *alutiqqutigaq*.

Many Aleuts still eat the traditional food of their ancestors. However, the Aleuts' diet began to change when they started trading goods with Europeans. They adopted foods such as bread and grains, various vegetables, and different meats. Today, Aleuts eat many of the same things most North Americans eat, while still enjoying many traditional foods from Aleut culture.

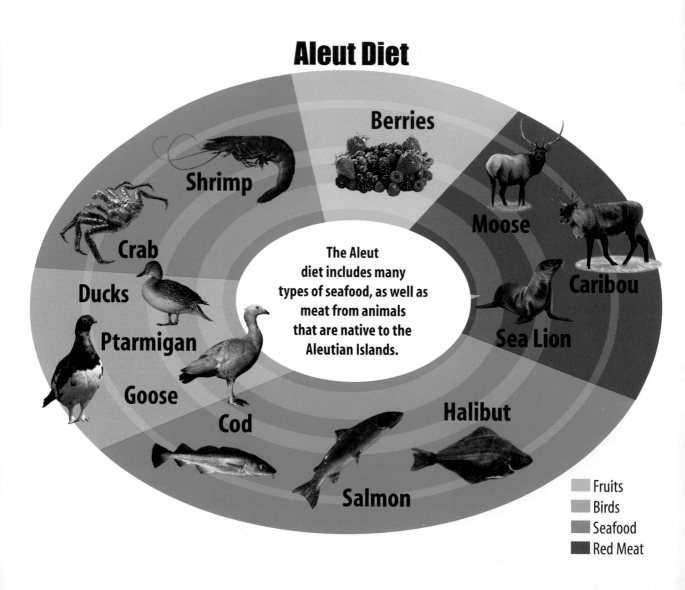

Aleut Diet

Berries

Shrimp

Crab

Ducks

Ptarmigan

Goose

Cod

Salmon

Halibut

Moose

Caribou

Sea Lion

The Aleut diet includes many types of seafood, as well as meat from animals that are native to the Aleutian Islands.

Fruits
Birds
Seafood
Red Meat

Salmon and other seafood are common in Aleut diet. Salmon is often caught, dried, and stored for winter months. The salmon fishing season runs from May through October each year.

The early Aleuts played many games, such as quoits and a stick and board game. Quoits was played on a green mat made from sealskin. Players tossed wooden rings at a bright strip painted down the middle of the mat. The player whose ring landed closest to the stripe scored a point. The stick and board game involved a thin wooden board with several holes carved in it. It was tied to the end of a sharp wooden stick. The player swings the board into the air and tries to "spear" it with the stick.

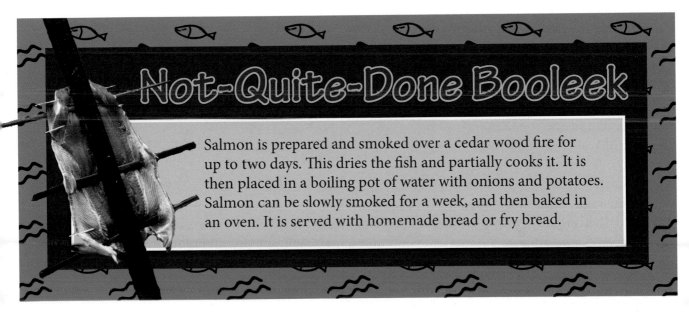

Not-Quite-Done Booleek

Salmon is prepared and smoked over a cedar wood fire for up to two days. This dries the fish and partially cooks it. It is then placed in a boiling pot of water with onions and potatoes. Salmon can be slowly smoked for a week, and then baked in an oven. It is served with homemade bread or fry bread.

Great Ideas

One of the most important aspects of Aleut life was hunting. Early Aleuts created many weapons and tools from stone, but most of their technology came from the sea. They created small sea **kayaks** called baidarkas. These were small skin boats made from sea lion skin. They were very sturdy and easy to maneuver. A one-man vessel was about 16 feet (4.9 meters) long and 20 inches (51 centimeters) wide. Large skin boats called baidara were used to travel from island to island. They could carry several people at once and were used to transport supplies for villages or warriors for battle.

Aleut hunters also developed several throwing weapons, such as spears, darts, and harpoons. The most widely used hunting weapon was the compound harpoon. This harpoon had a special stone tip made of two short pieces. After this tip entered an animal, the two short pieces would spread apart. This stopped the spear from falling out of the animal. It was an accurate and deadly hunting tool.

Hunting and fishing are both popular on the Aleutian Islands today. People hunt for big game such as reindeer, brown bears, and moose, and for small game such as ducks and geese. Trout, halibut, and different types of salmon are available in the waters surrounding the islands. While some Aleuts still use traditional hunting tools, such as spears, most use modern tools.

While hunting is still a popular sport in the Aleutian Islands, some animals, such as sea lions, are protected by law and cannot be hunted.

Early Aleuts crafted harpoons from walrus tusk ivory. They also used the material for other items, including sculpture and jewelry. They also carved sewing needles from ivory. These needles were custom made for individuals and often had the heads of animals, such as seals or whales, carved on them. Today, the U.S. government allows the Aleuts to harvest walrus ivory for use in crafts. They can sell these crafts as long as they follow certain regulations.

Barabaras

The rough weather of the far north forced the Aleut people to be very resourceful. They had to develop ways to live in such a cold and remote area. The early Aleuts built winter houses called barabaras. These underground houses were perfect for keeping the Aleuts dry, warm, and sheltered from the bitter winds of the Aleutian Islands. To build such houses, the Aleuts first dug a rectangular pit four or five feet (1.2 or 1.5 m) deep. A frame was built over the top with logs and poles. Then a layer of sod, dirt, and moss was laid over the frame. The Aleuts built a doorway into the roof. Inside were two rooms. The main room had benches to sit on and cots for children to sleep on. There were often several holes throughout the room used for toilets. A secondary room was reserved for the parents of the family.

At Issue

The Aleuts have faced many challenges throughout their history. They have faced the intrusion of European and American cultures. Many aspects of their own culture, language, religion, and political structures were suppressed or banned. Their traditional way of life was changed forever. They lost the freedom to hunt and fish, and were sometimes forced to work in the Russian fur trade instead. It has taken the Aleuts decades to rediscover their culture. Many laws are now in place that protect the basic human rights and culture of the Aleuts.

In the 1970s and 1980s, many environmental groups in the United States began to protest the seal hunts in the far north. They saw the killing of seals and their pups as inhumane and cruel. The Aleuts were unfairly targeted as being part of the problem. Seal hunting has been an important part of the Aleut culture for centuries. In 1983, the U.S. government decided to stop commercial seal hunting. It withdrew funding and protection of the industry in the Pribilof Islands. This left the Aleut people without any protection for their own seal hunting.

Aleuts balance their traditional values with their need for modern technology.

Older Aleuts strive to pass on traditions to the younger generations.

The Aleuts adapted quickly. They switched to fishing instead of seal hunting. They persuaded the federal government in Washington, DC, to invest $20 million into the area. They expanded their harbors to work with large fishing boats. Today, more than 100 local fishers work from these harbors.

There are many environmental issues facing the Aleut today. Increased fishing in the area has put a strain on the waterways and marine life. Fuel barges move millions of gallons (liters) of fuel a day through the largest and most sensitive wildlife area of the Southern Bering Sea. In March 1989, a vessel ran aground near the Pribilof Islands spilling 10,000 gallons (37,854 liters) of diesel fuel into the sea. This fuel polluted the waters and caused the death of a large number of king eider ducks. The tribal Aleut government sued the owners of the vessel and received an out-of-court settlement.

Aleutian Housing Authority

Some Aleutian people continue to face economic problems today. Besides unemployment and struggling industries like fishing, many Aleutians cannot find affordable housing. The Aleutian Housing Authority (AHA) was established in 1977 to provide inexpensive housing to low-income families in the Aleut community. In 1998, the federal Native American Housing and Self-Determination Act was passed. Since then, AHA has been servicing 12 federally recognized tribes throughout the islands. The group also works hard to create job training, employment, and economic development in the region.

Into the Future

The Aleut people have always been survivors. They have survived some of the harshest conditions on the planet. They also have survived the influence of outside cultures by adapting and working together to ensure their culture survives.

The Aleut of today are a fully modernized people. They live in modern houses, drive cars and trucks, and enjoy all the modern conveniences of North American life. They also maintain a link to their past by keeping their traditions and history alive. They pass these traditions to succeeding generations, so the Aleut way of life will live on.

The Aleuts have educated animal rights group about their responsible seal hunting practices. They fought for the right to take seal pelts for the making of traditional clothing and art work. They can now obtain and consume seal meat without harassment.

The Aleuts have created many social programs to deal with alcohol and drug abuse. Many fishing and food processing companies now have drug testing facilities. Anyone dealing with drug or alcohol addiction can get help at treatment facilities. Violent crime and crime related to drugs and alcohol is down in many Aleut communities in recent years.

Aleut leaders have responded to the challenges of the modern world. They have worked hard to find a balance between Western culture and their own traditions. Aleut people, such as Aquilina Bourdukofsky, began teaching Aleut tradition to younger generations in the early 1990s. Andrew Gronholdt was a famous Aleut artist responsible for bringing back the lost art of carving wood hats in the late 1980s. His techniques are taught to people today in workshops all over Alaska.

Aleut artists are keeping traditional arts and crafts alive.

Role-play Debate

When people debate a topic, two sides take a different viewpoint about one idea. Each side presents logical arguments to support its views. In a role-play debate, participants act out the roles of the key people or groups involved with the different viewpoints. Role-playing can build communication skills and help people understand how others may think and feel. Usually, each person or team is given a set amount of time to present its case. The participants take turns stating their arguments until the time set aside for the debate is up.

THE ISSUE

In the 1970s, groups like Greenpeace protested the hunting of seals for food and fur. They saw the practice as barbaric and cruel. Many private companies hunted seal for their fur. Unfortunately, the Aleut were targeted along with these commercial sealing companies. In 1985, the American government saw how unpopular the seal hunt was with many Americans. They decided to stop supporting the seal hunting industry. Many Aleuts had to change their way of life, giving up an important part of their culture. Today, several Aleut groups have reclaimed the right to hunt seal in accordance with their traditions. The number of seals they are permitted to hunt is, however, significantly lower.

THE QUESTION

Should the Aleuts be able to continue hunting seal and their young?

THE SIDES

NO

Animal Rights Activists:
The seal hunt is cruel and inhumane. Aleuts have other sources of food and clothing.

YES

Aleut Hunters: The seal hunt is an important part of Aleut culture. They rely on the seals for food and skins for traditional clothing and art.

Ready, Set, Go

Form two teams to debate the issue, and decide whether your team will play the role of the animal rights activists or the role of Aleuts. Each team should take time to use this book and other research to develop solid arguments for its side and to understand how the issue affects each group. At the end of the role-play debate, discuss how you feel after hearing both points of view.

World Cultures Quiz!

1 How many people can claim direct descent from the ancient Aleut?

2 What religion do most Aleuts follow today?

3 What is the name of the ancient belief system of the Aleuts?

4 When did the first Paleo-Aleuts arrive from the Alaskan mainland?

5 What year did Danish explorer Vitus Bering discover the Aleutian Islands?

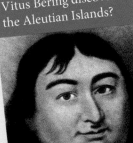

6 How do you say hello in Aleut?

7 What is the Aleut traditional wooden hunting hat called?

8 What is the name of the Aleut sea kayak?

9 What was the name of the traditional Aleut house built half-underground?

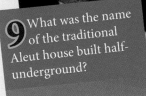

10 Most Aleut people have switched from seal hunting to what industry?

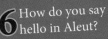

ANSWER KEY

1. 2000 2. Russian Orthodoxy
3. Animism 4. Around 2000 BC
5. 1741 6. Aang 7. A chaguda-x
8. A baidarka 9. Barabara
10. Fishing

Key Words

archaeologists: scientists who study prehistoric humans and their culture throughout history

blubber: fat from whales and other sea animals

climate change: Change in average weather conditions over a period of time caused by chemical, biological, geological, atmospheric, and other changes

converting: the act of inspiring or convincing someone to follow another religion other than their own

dialect: a particular form of language

indigenous: originating in a particular place, native to an area

internment: being placed against your will in a secured camp during wartime

jurisdiction: the power, right, or control of a government

kayaks: small sea boats

missionaries: people sent to areas to promote a particular religion

mummified: used to describe a body that is dried an preserved

parka: a wind proof jacket with a hood

pelts: the skins of animals with fur still on them

revolt: to rebel or rise against authority

sinew: a piece of tough tissue that connects muscle or bone

visor: a stiff bill on the front of a hat

Index

Log on to www.av2books.com

AV² by Weigl brings you media enhanced books that support active learning. Go to www.av2books.com, and enter the special code found on page 2 of this book. You will gain access to enriched and enhanced content that supplements and complements this book. Content includes video, audio, weblinks, quizzes, a slide show, and activities.

AV² Online Navigation

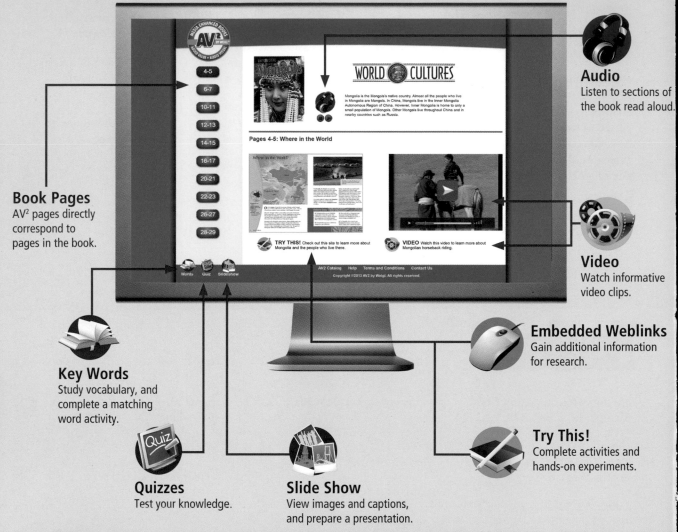

Book Pages
AV² pages directly correspond to pages in the book.

Audio
Listen to sections of the book read aloud.

Video
Watch informative video clips.

Key Words
Study vocabulary, and complete a matching word activity.

Embedded Weblinks
Gain additional information for research.

Try This!
Complete activities and hands-on experiments.

Quizzes
Test your knowledge.

Slide Show
View images and captions, and prepare a presentation.

AV² was built to bridge the gap between print and digital. We encourage you to tell us what you like and what you want to see in the future.

Sign up to be an AV² Ambassador at www.av2books.com/ambassador.

Due to the dynamic nature of the Internet, some of the URLs and activities provided as part of AV² by Weigl may have changed or ceased to exist. AV² by Weigl accepts no responsibility for any such changes. All media enhanced books are regularly monitored to update addresses and sites in a timely manner. Contact AV² by Weigl at 1-866-649-3445 or av2books@weigl.com with any questions, comments, or feedback.